preppy
coloring book

Hello There!

Thank you so much for purchasing this book. We recommend using pencils to ensure that you have the best experience with this coloring book and if you are going to use any type of ink that may cause bleeding our suggestion is to tear out the coloring pages or use buffer pages between the papers (blank buffer pages can be found at the end of the book).
Also if you enjoy it, then please leave an Amazon review. Reviews are the lifeblood of our publishing endeavors and leaving a positive review would mean the world to us.

Sincerely,

Zio Alca

In order to prevent color bleeding, this page has been intentionally left blank.

In order to prevent color bleeding, this page has been intentionally left blank.

In order to prevent color bleeding, this page has been intentionally left blank.

In order to prevent color bleeding, this page has been intentionally left blank.

In order to prevent color bleeding, this page has been intentionally left blank.

In order to prevent color bleeding, this page has been intentionally left blank.

In order to prevent color bleeding, this page has been intentionally left blank.

In order to prevent color bleeding, this page has been intentionally left blank.

In order to prevent color bleeding, this page has been intentionally left blank.

In order to prevent color bleeding, this page has been intentionally left blank.

In order to prevent color bleeding, this page has been intentionally left blank.

In order to prevent color bleeding, this page has been intentionally left blank.

In order to prevent color bleeding, this page has been intentionally left blank.

In order to prevent color bleeding, this page has been intentionally left blank.

In order to prevent color bleeding, this page has been intentionally left blank.

In order to prevent color bleeding, this page has been intentionally left blank.

In order to prevent color bleeding, this page has been intentionally left blank.

In order to prevent color bleeding, this page has been intentionally left blank.

In order to prevent color bleeding, this page has been intentionally left blank.

In order to prevent color bleeding, this page has been intentionally left blank.

In order to prevent color bleeding, this page has been intentionally left blank.

In order to prevent color bleeding, this page has been intentionally left blank.

In order to prevent color bleeding, this page has been intentionally left blank.

In order to prevent color bleeding, this page has been intentionally left blank.

In order to prevent color bleeding, this page has been intentionally left blank.

In order to prevent color bleeding, this page has been intentionally left blank.

In order to prevent color bleeding, this page has been intentionally left blank.

In order to prevent color bleeding, this page has been intentionally left blank.

In order to prevent color bleeding, this page has been intentionally left blank.

In order to prevent color bleeding, this page has been intentionally left blank.

In order to prevent color bleeding, this page has been intentionally left blank.

In order to prevent color bleeding, this page has been intentionally left blank.

In order to prevent color bleeding, this page has been intentionally left blank.

In order to prevent color bleeding, this page has been intentionally left blank.

In order to prevent color bleeding, this page has been intentionally left blank.

In order to prevent color bleeding, this page has been intentionally left blank.

In order to prevent color bleeding, this page has been intentionally left blank.

In order to prevent color bleeding, this page has been intentionally left blank.

In order to prevent color bleeding, this page has been intentionally left blank.

In order to prevent color bleeding, this page has been intentionally left blank.

In order to prevent color bleeding, this page has been intentionally left blank.

In order to prevent color bleeding, this page has been intentionally left blank.

In order to prevent color bleeding, this page has been intentionally left blank.

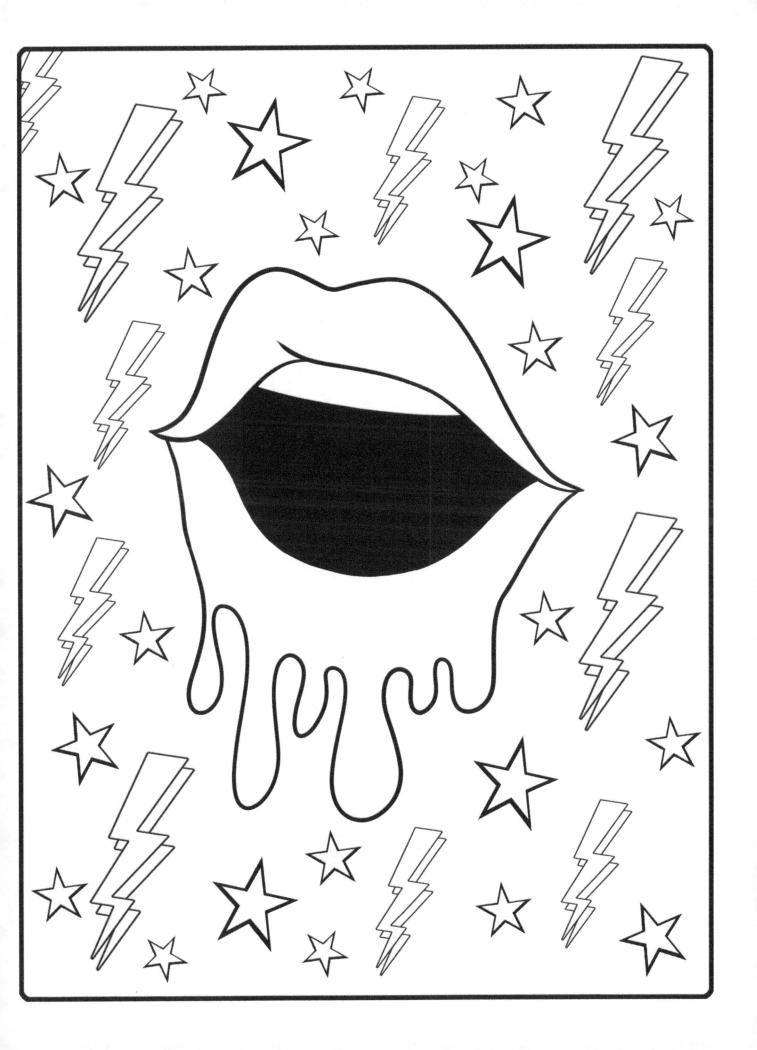

In order to prevent color bleeding, this page has been intentionally left blank.

In order to prevent color bleeding, this page has been intentionally left blank.

In order to prevent color bleeding, this page has been intentionally left blank.

In order to prevent color bleeding, this page has been intentionally left blank.

In order to prevent color bleeding, this page has been intentionally left blank.

In order to prevent color bleeding, this page has been intentionally left blank.

In order to prevent color bleeding, this page has been intentionally left blank.

Buffer Paper

If you are using any ink that may bleed, please cut this buffer paper and use it between pages.

This page has been intentionally left blank.

Buffer Paper
If you are using any ink that may bleed,
please cut this buffer paper and use it
between pages.

This page has been intentionally left blank.

Made in the USA
Monee, IL
28 June 2025